Two Girls and ⁝

Rosie Jackson has a first-class degree in English & Comparative Literature from the University of Warwick, a DPhil from York, and has taught in many educational settings, including the University of East Anglia, Nottingham Trent, UWE Bristol, Skyros Writers' Lab, Cortijo Romero, and the Open College of the Arts. Her poetry is published in *Acumen*, *Ambit*, *Domestic Cherry*, *Frogmore Papers*, *High Window*, *Poetry Ireland Review*, *Poetry Salzburg Review*, *Scintilla*, *Tears in the Fence*, *The Interpreter's House*, and other journals and anthologies, has been set for GCSE and used for a sculpture by Andrew Whittle in the grounds of a Dorchester hospital. She was a Hawthornden fellow in 2017. Awards include 1st prize Poetry Space 2019, 1st prize at Wells 2018 and 1st prize in the Stanley Spencer Poetry Competition 2017. Rosie lives in Frome, Somerset, where she teaches creative writing workshops.

www.rosiejackson.org.uk

Graham Burchell has lived and worked in Zambia, Saudi Arabia, Tenerife, Mexico, France, Chile and the United States. He was a teacher from 1976 to 2003, with a BEd in Art and Education. He became a full-time writer in 2004 and gained an MA in Creative Writing from Bath Spa University in 2010. His poetry has appeared in most of the major UK poetry magazines and he has won, been placed or commended in many competitions, including 1st prize in the Red Shed Poetry Competition, 2018, 3rd place in Bridport 2017, runner-up in the 2016 BBC Proms poetry competition, 1st prize in the National Stanza Competition 2015 and 2012 Canterbury Festival Poet of the Year. He was a Hawthornden fellow in 2013. Now living in South Devon, he is active in the Devon poetry scene and one of the team running the Teignmouth Poetry Festival.

www.gburchell.com

By the same authors

Rosie Jackson

Fantasy: The Literature of Subversion, Methuen (1981)
The Eye of the Buddha and Other Therapeutic Tales, Women's Press (1991)
Frieda Lawrence, Harper Collins (1994)
Mothers Who Leave, Harper Collins (1994)
What the Ground Holds, Poetry Salzburg (2014)
The Light Box, Cultured Llama (2016)
The Glass Mother: A Memoir, Unthank (2016)
Aloneness is a Many-headed Bird (with Dawn Gorman),
    Hedgehog Press (2020)

Graham Burchell

Vermeer's Corner, Foothills Publishing, NY (2008)
The Chongololo Club, Pindrop Press (2012)
Kate, Indigo Dreams (2015)
Cottage Pi, SPM Publications, Sentinel (2015)
Breakfast under a Yellow-Bellied Sun, Indigo Dreams (2018)

Also by Two Rivers Poets

William Bedford, *The Dancers of Colbek* (2020)
Kate Behrens, *Penumbra* (2019)
Conor Carville, *English Martyrs* (2019)
John Froy, *Sandpaper & Seahorses* (2018)
Maria Teresa Horta, *Point of Honour* translated by Lesley Saunders (2019)
Ian House, *Just a Moment* (2020)
Sue Leigh, *Chosen Hill* (2018)
James Peake, *Reaction Time of Glass* (2019)
Peter Robinson & David Inshaw, *Bonjour Mr Inshaw* (2020)
Peter Robinson, *The Constitutionals: A Fiction* (2019)
Lesley Saunders, *Nominy-Dominy* (2018)
Jack Thacker, *Handling* (2018)
Jean Watkins, *Precarious Lives* (2018)

Two Girls and a Beehive

Poems about the art and lives
of Stanley Spencer
and Hilda Carline Spencer

Rosie Jackson & Graham Burchell

dear Ruthie –

" to taste the wonder of ourselves "

love

Rosie

June 2020

TWO
RIVERS
PRESS

First published in the UK in 2020 by Two Rivers Press
7 Denmark Road, Reading RG1 5PA.
www.tworiverspress.com

ISBN 978-1-909747-59-3

1 2 3 4 5 6 7 8 9

Two Rivers Press is represented in the UK by Inpress Ltd
and distributed by NBNi.

Front cover image Stanley Spencer's *Two Girls and a Beehive*,
1910 (oil on canvas), © The Estate of Stanley Spencer/Bridgeman Images

Text design by Nadja Guggi and typeset in Janson and Parisine

Printed and bound in Great Britain by Imprint Digital, Exeter

Acknowledgements

We would like to thank the editors of the following publications in whose journals and anthologies some of these poems first appeared: *Acumen*; *Domestic Cherry*; *High Window*; *Ink, Sweat and Tears*; *Long Poem Magazine*; *Mary Evans Picture Library*; *New Welsh Review*; *Poetry and All That Jazz*; *Poetry Salzburg Review*; *Pratik: A Magazine of Contemporary Writing*; *Stanley Spencer Poems: An Anthology* (Two Rivers Press 2017); *The Eye that Looks* (University of Reading Creative Arts Anthology 2019); also in Rosie Jackson's *What the Ground Holds* (Poetry Salzburg, 2014) and *The Light Box* (Cultured Llama, 2016).

Thanks to the judges and organisers of the poetry competitions in which some of the poems were placed. 'A Loss of Eden' won 1st prize in the Red Shed Poetry Competition, 2018; 'What Is Beautiful I do not Know' won 2nd prize at Torbay Poetry Festival, 2018; 'The Heaven that Runs through Everything' won 1st prize in Cookham Festival's Stanley Spencer Poetry Competition, 2017; 'A Ward Sister Remembers the Spencers' won 3rd prize in the Hippocrates Open Competition, 2017; 'John Donne Arriving in Heaven' won joint 1st prize at Bath Poetry Café, 2015; 'Resurrection: Reunion' won 2nd prize in the Acumen and Bath Poetry Competition, 2012.

We are very grateful to Professor David Morley, Annie Freud and Anthony Thwaite for endorsements, Professor Peter Robinson and Sally Mortimore at Two Rivers Press for their support, Claire Dyer for insightful editing, and our vibrant poetry communities in Somerset and Devon for critiques and encouragement.

Many excellent publications helped us source our material, including: Keith Bell, *Stanley Spencer* (Phaidon, 1992); Maurice Collis, *Stanley Spencer: A Biography* (Harvill Press, London, 1962); Adrian Glew, *Stanley Spencer: Letters and Writings* (Tate Gallery, London, 2001); Stanley Spencer, *Looking to Heaven* (Unicorn Press, 2016); Unity Spencer, *Lucky to be an Artist* (Unicorn Press, 2015); Alison Thomas, *The Art of Hilda Carline* (Lincolnshire County Council, 1999).

We are especially grateful to John Spencer, grandson of Stanley and Hilda, for his permission to reproduce quotations and writings from letters and diaries owned by the Spencer estate and for his support of our project.

Contents

I. A Village in Heaven

II. Portrait of the Artist with Two Wives

III. Summer Without Fire

IV. Hilda with Bluebells

V. Love's Return

All paintings referred to are by Stanley Spencer unless otherwise stated. They are readily available to view on the Internet.

'I like my life so much that I would like to cover every empty space on a wall with it. Painting pictures is my way of giving praise: I don't know to whom... When I paint a picture I am building an altar.'

—Stanley Spencer, November 1922

'To a creative person making things of some sort or kind is essential.'

—Hilda Carline Spencer

'To a large extent the problems of poets are the problems of painters, and poets must often turn to the literature of painting for a discussion of their own problems.'

—Wallace Stevens, *Adagia*

I. A Village in Heaven

Two Girls and a Beehive

after 'Two Girls and a Beehive', 1910

He has these butcher's daughters
(both ginger-haired as honeycomb and sunset),
smelling roses, just that, as if oblivious
to the hovering of the holy ghost behind
and that box of whispering bees.

He loved them both, those Wooster girls,
dressed them in shades of privet green,
gave them an evening glow and posed them
on puddles of light; the last gold lily-pads
of the day.
                At times they would sit, Dot
and Emmie, on his garden wall, chatter
and giggle, backs against black railings,
and hedge of that same viridian hue.

Perhaps he felt himself to be
supernatural as he watched
from the nursery window, thinking,
I can look and linger on you my two loves,
but you cannot see me.

But what of the bees, the honey-makers
in their Mill Lane hive? He paints them at rest,
contained, still as evening, a potential
for both sweetness and pain.
Just that.

Oh!

'I like saying 'oh' because it does not mean anything
and yet is so expressive of what I feel.'
—Stanley Spencer, Letter written at Applehayes, Clayhidon,
 Devon, 1911

Oh Mr Tonks, formidable drawing master at The Slade,
why did you send the boy far across the country?
Back at home, brother Sydney shook his head.
No, no that won't work, he said.

Stanley, aged twenty who'd never spent
a night away from home, fretted and sweated
in the summer heat of Applehayes.
Everything was old: house, fireplaces, beams,

pathetic farm labourer... Stanley drew him in red chalk,
he who'd finished work early being so hot,
looking so ill. Here was a face slashed and beaten
by the English outdoors.

Here was a face divisible – *like a jigsaw puzzle*, Stanley said,
his arms burning under the sun as he sketched,
burning when he strolled. He could walk anywhere,
it all belonged, fields, bracken, bramble –

nobody else about, no-one! This was a desert,
his Berkshire idyll, paradise. Back there,
he believed it would kill him if he left again.

Back there, he wanted to draw all the good folk
of the village; to begin at one end, work through –
people, people everywhere.

Cowls

after 'Mending Cowls, Cookham', 1915

They swivel above their oasthouses
among the geometry of rooftops:
white wooden heads looking, listening,
curious reminders of a religious presence.

Among the geometry of rooftops
he observes them from the nursery window,
curious reminders of a religious presence
in this time of war.

He observes them from the nursery window.
They sometimes veer towards him
in this time of war,
as if to say, *have no part in it.*

They sometimes veer towards him,
but today he notes the cowls are still,
as if to say, *we'll have no part in it.*
He wants to paint them being fixed.

But today he notes the cowls are still,
tipped up or opened with men inside.
He wants to paint them being fixed,
these wooden angels, accessible, desanctified,

tipped up or opened with men inside.
He paints a dark foreboding sky above
these wooden angels, accessible, desanctified,
their inner emptiness exposed.

He paints a dark foreboding sky above.
Later, he will say the painting depresses him,
the inner emptiness exposed,
and complain that it looks like some other place.

Later, he will say the picture depresses him,
even though it's one of his most religious,
and he'll complain that it looks like some other place.
He won't know how to bear it,

even though it's one of his most religious,
white wooden heads looking, listening.
He won't know how to bear it. Still
they swivel above their oasthouses.

Of Angels and Dirt

'I am on the side of the angels and dirt.'
—Stanley Spencer

God, he's sure, does not have preferences,
does not value the sky above the earth,
nor winged things over grit in the wayside.
While you're craning your neck, scanning the clouds
for some moment of white revelation,
an epiphany that's always off-stage,
he's sketching these torn leaves of wild rhubarb
in the gravel beneath an old stone wall,
capturing in Pre-Raphaelite detail
their miracles of ribbing, chlorophyll,
time-travelled light, unheard-of frequencies.

Chiaroscuro

after 'Self-Portrait', 1914

How smooth he was then, lit
as if by campfire flames with his strong neck
and light flop of fringe – quite a catch,
but with green still showing through.

He painted himself that way,
with the suggestion of warrior male
because he was twenty three.
His country had gone to war. A reddening

to the whites of his eyes suggests weariness,
his conscience giving him no peace.
He thought he might join a civic guard,
be drilled without being in the army.

In the barber's, a family man
joining up for the second time, going
the very next day, told Stanley
that he should be. *Why aren't you?*

That was like a prod with a bayonet,
leaving him feeling foolish, a lout
when he saw his parted-hair reflection
in the mirror.

Late spring light paled his skin.
There was no bold chiaroscuro here, or outside
on a Cookham street, where each wind-blown
flip-flap of a trouser leg spelled guilt.

July is a Dry Month

July is a dry month, he says.
He's spread no paint across taut canvases.
Everything is war and emptiness.

The village has lost its youth, its way.
His half painted Swan Upping must wait. Yes,
July is a dry month, he says.

And mother's attitude has softened these days.
He can leave, suspend his art, his flapping swans, his…
Everything is war and emptiness.

Perhaps they'll send him to Bristol (vile place),
vile hospital with bed pans, blood, bandages…
July is a dry month, he says.

He'd prefer to be a Tommy in battle dress,
join the Berkshires, indulge their practices,
when everything is war and emptiness.

He thinks he'll have to scrub the lavs, the mess,
but there'll be no front line disadvantages.
July is a dry month, he says
now everything is war and emptiness.

Roaring Great Hospital

after 'Convoy of Wounded Soldiers
Arriving at Beaufort Hospital Gates', 1927

It was a lunatic asylum with rain, a driveway
dressed with wax dark leaves of rhododendron,
the gates closed.
                            But he paints them being opened
in sunshine, oiled and recoated in terracotta red.

It was a lunatic asylum with sixteen hundred beds.
They moved the patients to the country,
held back eighty for domestic duties.

And now a flat-nosed, children's book bus idles
with its bloody cargo: that sanguineous mess, hidden
under bandages, triangles of white slings
pulled together like a trawl of clattering sailing boats,
dragged through a channel of flowers;

hundreds of men who barely perceive softness,
long shadows, or notice how birdsong
chimes louder than any complaint.

He, a barely known genius, fits in as an orderly,
says he's done nothing but scrub since he got here.
He believes it's done him some good.

Macedonia, 1918

One day, back in Cookham, he will turn this into pattern
and meaning: mules pulling travoys of the wounded
to a nativity barn of a makeshift theatre,

snow-capped peaks rising through flat cloud
above magenta beauty. He will paint
a whole church full of redemption.

But for now, weak from malaria, he stands
in stiff boots watching purple skies, stars
clinging to the skirts of a swollen moon.

Orchards do not exist here, or children.
The mountains are boulders waiting to be rolled away,
the war a Jericho of massacres asking not to happen.

Then music rises like the river Moses struck out of rock,
cascading down the walls of disbelief,
and for a blessed hour the awful empty silence recedes.

He can hear again Bach's Preludes: the ones his brother,
Sydney, handsome, upright Sydney, would play
in the drawing room by guttering candle-light.

And later, when he hears that Sydney's died
in France, one of 17 million souls in the war's
bloody ledger, he will remember this moment,

clinging to every note as if it were twilight
in Cookham and this the last blackbird's song
striking bone again and again behind his temples.

He will remember the books on his crate of a table,
Shakespeare, Milton, Marvell, Keats, Blake –
manna in the wilderness of the Balkans –

and Crashaw, Richard Crashaw, whose lines
hold him like the pews of a church,
somewhere to sit, pray, ponder.

He will remember the vow he's made today –
how he'll devote himself to art once he's home,
put sky back onto the world, paint Berkshire

as if it's some bucolic scene by Claude Lorrain,
all orange and lilac light, cows crossing streams,
fresh-faced men and women dancing.

And he will liken man to a tortoise, tasked
with impossible distances, God to a snake charmer
wanting to see what we're made of.

Travoys with Wounded Soldiers

after 'Travoys with Wounded Soldiers Arriving
at a Dressing Station at Smol, Macedonia', 1919

There is part truth in what you see.
The ruined mosque, brightly lit
like a bad dream nativity scene
or a macabre lock-up,
re-imagined by an artist up a tree,
is how he shows it. It's not how it was,
everything brown charred almost to black,
lightened almost to dirty white,
brightened to blood red – almost.
The fan of horses at the entrance
trailing cargoes of hurt men,
as if delivered for divine healing,
or as meat for medical experimentation,
was not how it was at Smol, not quite.
What you have here is a silent night
without agonies or hoof clopping.
There's nothing left of the clatter
of steel-tipped travoys that rode stones
and potholes: so profound, that years later,
any sudden metallic sound invoked
the memory, brought back those nights,
the sight and smell of tortoises,
seen on the way up, charred ghost white
by grass fire.

A Loss of Eden

after 'Swan Upping at Cookham', 1915–19

Four Cookham winters have passed.
His canvas was stretched and at ease when he primed it,
when Mrs Grimsdale still had her sons
and Guy Lacey's dog, Tinker, was just a pup.

It's 1919. He's lost that early morning feeling
which so awakened his spirit. He used to spring
from his bed, light-limbed and ready. Not any more.
It seems improper, less than sensible to paint again.

There's such a hush. Even engines, voices
and complaining swans seem muffled.
How can the king's vintners and dyers swan-up,
as if it's just another July?

In church, kneeling with head bowed and eyes closed,
half in prayer, half tuning to outside sounds,
he catches voices, the sweat and rush, snatching
and marking.

Before, he'd imagined his river dark and cold,
the sky and far riverbanks darker. Now, he needs
to let in some light, lighten foreground ripples
into furrows of mauve. He needs to part the clouds.

Red Brick

'I like to take my thoughts for a walk and marry them
to some place in Cookham.'
—Stanley Spencer

How many ivy-free walls did he paint, knowing
he loved to spread the terracotta of himself
and stripe it with mortar lines?

How sunny and homely did it make him feel
to frame biblical moments within brick verticals,
placing cut-out familiars, turning, tilting, jamming
them together liked meshed bars on a typewriter?

Which shopkeepers, friends, sweethearts did he dress
to be the magi, to waggle toes under the table
at *The Last Supper*, to be *The Daughters of Jerusalem*?

We believe they became *The Builders*, *Adorers of Old Men*,
old men. He looked down on them as they looked up
to God in their long socks, rolled up sleeves, tweeds,
floral and patterned skirts and white beards.

He gave us *Christ's Entry into Jerusalem* – except it wasn't.
Our lord was hurrying towards pavement and railings
near the artist's home – red brick with sun on it.

He loved to hem them, herd them. Hemmed himself
with a swan-like mistress in fur at the back of the house,
with a smaller himself as observer: almost all of it
tinted mud red as brick and tile.

Take This Pink Cookham Morning

after 'Christ Carrying the Cross', 1920

When you rise out of yourself you could be anywhere –
crawling from a chest of drawers, climbing
from beneath that stone by your own front door.

You could be walking down the street wiping sleep
from your eyes, pass men in grey with their ritual caps,
boys who grip railings like spears.

You could be squashed at one of the windows
in garrets, bedrooms, homes choked with ivy,
your flimsy lace curtains like wings.

You could be watching a carpenter, the white wood
he carries as tall as a cross, or dodging the ladders
of two men behind him, nimble as thieves.

You could pinch yourself at this vision you can't quite believe,
the way those fields on the village edge hold something
you've never known: a glimpse of heaven

leaking its light backwards – a radiance out of the frame
that makes everything see-through, newly fledged –
the sky lapis, the landscape of light so clear, undoing,

you press palms over your eyes to protect
against dazzle and glare. Never more yourself
than when you leave behind all you thought you were.

What Ho, Giotto

'What Ho, Giotto,' Stanley Spencer's exclamation
on hearing that the Behrends had agreed to sponsor
the chapel at Burghclere in 1927.

'...ever busy, yet ever at rest...'
—St Augustine

He turns to paint frescoes like Giotto's in Padua,
but transfigures the blatantly biblical
into moments of calm in a great war:

men washing lockers in magenta baths.
He likes the colour – paints himself tucked
between two of them. Their shapes loom.

His protective sacking is a prayer mat.
Once seen, it presents a shift from the material
to the spiritual. That's his way,

but don't tell the bishop until after
the chapel's dedication. He may not grasp
the intent, that the act of doing describes God;

the Augustinian nod to fetching and carrying,
coming and going, scrubbing, sorting...
They're stuffed full of religion, apparently.

The linings, the dermis of his Holy Box,
the Oratory of All Souls,
this Sandham Memorial Chapel

with its arched panels, predellas, panoramas,
and a chaos of crosses with resurrecting soldiers,
offers the mundane, the traffic of war damage:

the fixing of frost bites, ripping soiled sheets
from beds, sorting laundry, sorting, mending,
filling urns and pouring cups of tea.

II. Portrait of the Artist
with Two Wives

What is Beautiful I do not Know

after Hilda Carline Spencer's 'Melancholy in a Country Garden', 1921

Shortly before Dürer drew *Melencolia I*, he wrote:
'What is beautiful I do not know...'

She has not read Freud's *Mourning and Melancholia*,
but likes the term melancholy for lowness of spirits.
It makes her think of windows so small

even the sun has to struggle to enter. She remembers
Dürer's *Melencolia Imaginativa*, that sombre seated woman
not-lost-in-babies and Italian beaches, but facing it all:

the hour-glass, the nothing-lasts. Melancholy gives meaning
to her slight stoop, her eventual impatience with Stanley's
exuberance, her need for gardens and equilibrium.

Melancholy doesn't ask for pills but for prayer,
the comfort of a Christian Science manual, a philosophy
that says hammer and nails are all part of the divine plan.

She paints trees rooted deep in the water-table, green leaves
which will not blazon butcher-red, and in their midst a woman
seen from behind, her coat long and dark even in summer.

In the Train to Sarajevo

after 'Sarajevo', 1922

they slept together, side by side, head to toe,
fully dressed. He remembers the electricity,
what she was wearing (a grey dress and a coat
with grey braid), and he reflects on their first meeting,
when his collar stud broke.

In the train to Sarajevo they were tucked away
in a corner, not seen, and they could look at each other
without innocence or awkwardness. In the city
she took his arm; that small press of reassurance
into a sleeve.

In the city he painted what he saw, a minaret
reaching for the sky, the hills and valleys of Yugoslavia
in soft greys behind.
                    Back in Hampstead, as he passed
her open bedroom door, he glimpsed one naked leg.

What Else Did They Do?

When they weren't painting, making love,
talking about God, sex, or money, what else
did they do? Did they shop together, argue
over beef or ham, compete to roll out
the thinnest pastry? Did they stay up all night
to chart the shades of darkness, marvel
at the resurrection of the light? Did they
measure their daughter's foot against a matchbox,
study weather vanes, read different reds
across the early morning sky? Did they relish
the sound of the other's name, or their own,
as they were whispered on the pillow, *Stanley,*
Hilda? Did they lie down in bluebell woods,
cushioned by fresh bracken, stare up
through translucent leaves at catkins,
blackbirds? Did they tell each other jokes,
laugh out of control, decide that, in the beginning,
God must have laughed so much he split his ribs
and the universe floated out of his side
before he could stop it? Did they calculate
the odds of their meeting, promise
they would find each other in any after life,
push aside saints, angels, even God himself
as soon as they caught sight of those familiar
shoulders, that precious head? Did they love
the smell of fresh bread, parkin, lavender?
Did they get tired one afternoon, leaning
on the fence at Chapel View, notice the grass
on the other side was an extraordinary green,
the same emerald they might find in Paradise?

Photograph, 1928

From a photo showing Spencer with his first wife, Hilda,
their daughter, Shirin, his future wife Patricia, and friends,
picnicking near Cookham

Here it is in black and white – the moment
when the penny should have dropped.
Patricia's sleeveless dress, its large bow
asking to be undone, Stanley perched
almost in her lap, as close as he would be
nine years later in *The Leg of Mutton Nude*.
Shirin has overturned a flask of tea,
and the eight grown-ups could be chess
pieces on the board of Odney Common.
Stanley plays King, Patricia is elevated
from pawn to new white queen,
and Hilda now sees she herself is to be
toppled in a few deft moves.

Why don't the rooks, knights, bishops
intervene? There's her mother, all spine
and ostrich plumes, Richard Hartley
and two timid men whose names
she has forgotten. Perhaps they consider
a genius is allowed to make a fool of himself.
Perhaps they think light simply rearranges
matter, and all their spirits look down
from a higher plane which gives
this game some meaning.

But the worst shame is the sight of herself
eyeing the camera in her short-sleeved blouse –
cuckquean, the wife who knows but cannot stop
her husband's wandering. Her floppy straw hat
heralds the silly headgear Stanley will wear

on his second wedding day, along with glasses
thick as swimming goggles, as if he knows
he's out of his depth with Patricia,
but no longer cares, and all he'd once called love,
or homecoming, has been plunged underwater.

Lady in Green

after Hilda Carline Spencer's 'Portrait of Patricia Preece', 1933

She must like butter, Hilda thinks,
for her skin has that buttercup glow
as if she's rolled all morning in a meadow
of wild flowers and is covered in pollen.

Hilda's palette is limited,
she doesn't like the muddy browns
of mistrust, but paints people as if light
were spread equally inside them,

as if it were possible to capture the soul
in its invisible perfection, as clear
as water, able to run into any shape.
But she knows how yellow turns to green

in the shadow and has to push away
the thought of what Patricia has
that she doesn't – her husband's longing,
a certain knack with necklaces and hats.

She mixes canal green for Patricia's blouse,
starts on the string of glass beads
Stanley probably bought.
If her canvas were a mirror, she thinks,

she might catch sight of her own tall soul
standing behind her,
watching over her shoulder,
solemnly wringing its hands.

Portrait of the Artist with Two Wives

after Spencer's 'Portrait of Patricia Preece', 1933

You might think a man
would not want his past
and future wives to meet

but here they are,
one painting the other,
as intimate as chopsticks.

He decides to paint Patricia
too, heavy-boned, sitting
in front of a wind-up gramophone

where she glowers,
her hair the colour
of ripe hay.

Later, he tries to remember
what the gramophone
was playing -

Ethel Waters' 'Stormy Weather',
perhaps, or *I'm in the money*,
'The Gold Digger's Song'.

Patricia Preece

after 'Patricia at Cockmarsh Hill', 1935

erupts into a rough of white yarrow
like a mole hill, like a mole
with hair less velvet, and lighter,
the colour of bracken,

and with such hands, rakers,
shovers, gold-digging forepaws,
one digit bearing a ring
set with diamonds, that sparkle

against the shadow of her *à la mode*
choker necklace, like a zip pull
that she feels for to change her head
for another more appropriate to the season.

She cannot play Persephone today,
summer is already well advanced.
Hawthorns in their working-girl dresses
dot this hillside as if waiting for a chord
to kick off a country dance.
                                        No,
she'll need to search her bag of heads
for one with larger, paler eyes.

Before she gets to her feet to step
with trepidation up the track with him,
she'll need her vulnerable head on, the one
which paints her hungry for his attention.

Madonna Lilies

after 'Madonna Lilies', 1935

Summer shadows – peace.
There's nothing more to hear beyond insects,
brush strokes and a man's gentle breathing.

There must be people close by,
but at this moment, in this frame,
there are none.

He paints the silence of a blistered white-painted trellis,
and a tricycle waiting for the energy
of its small rider.

He gives us no sky, shows no seeds of the notions
that will be flawed enough to crack
and break marriages.

No, here's just the sex and scent of open-petalled
Madonna lilies beside deflowered poppy heads.
Here's an artist bathing

in familiar glory days as June tips into July,
with little thought beyond the placement
of those shadows,

the incarnation of utter Englishness (blessed Cookham),
and a thickening of his wallet. Later –
It is finished Mr Tooth. Please sell this to a private buyer,
not a gallery. This is not my true art.

And another stillness ensues, a lengthy pause,
like a lily's stamens between the tickle of bees,
before this moment on canvas is sold
to a gallery in Leeds.

Meadow

after 'By the River', 1935

He stains everything gold for a time of day
he loves to paint; that out-flowing tide of light.
And he puts himself in the middle of it all,
hands thrust deep into trouser pockets
below a striped jacket. He breathes in the perfume
of a fur coat wrapped about his shoulders and mouth.

Is the coat Patricia's? Is that her, foreground-large,
lying like a balsa manikin, holding out a letter?
An invitation? A notice of separation?
And are those his children sharing the space,
the elder, Shirin, looking away, slightly disconsolate,
and the younger, Unity, clutching her uncle's knee?
Is that Richard Carline, Stanley's alter-ego,
the perfect father, staring into the shadows,
thrusting a gathered spray of meadow towards Stanley?

The meadow, this tract of wildness rough-edging
the river behind Cookham's High Street,
is enlivened with petals and tags of childhood –
names he used to sound like sighs –
marsh mallow, bell flower, ragged robin, cranesbill.
Plants mostly left at peace, but jostled
on summer evenings like this, after church,
by those who like to come, sit and be.

Elsie

after 'Washing Up', 1935

the maid (country girl), sat the children in a kitchen drawer.
There they could watch her iron, wash up, dry her hands,
those that chopped untrimmed wood that came in *puffs* –
bundles.

He drew her tugging twigs, holding a branch vertically
to divide the symmetry of her white-aproned black dress,
her body scrunched like something not ironed.

He liked the way she picked stockings from the washing line,
grabbing the feet several at a time to make a fan,
and unpegged them, so they fell across her arms or shoulders
like slaughtered animals.

As he looked to his sketch pad, made marks, she told him
that years before she walked great distances to school:
simple hardy routines, trudging, picking, washing up.

He painted her in the kitchen, heavenly in a worldly setting,
wiping those chapped hands on a roller towel.
He added himself drying brushes, and Hilda, hair in a bun,
stretching to return a saucepan to the top shelf.

So many hands in this. His daughter Shirin pushes the corner
of a teacloth around a saucer. She looks unhappy,
bothered by the dishes; a tower of Babel before her.

Going to Bed

after 'Going to Bed', 1936

Finding a way on to the sacred hills of our parents' bed
was joyous: warmth and musk, soft sugarloaf lifts
and lady valleys; we two sisters, grabbing and sliding
in the same skin that was born from their union,

we two, exploring a shifting geography
of leaf-patterned eiderdown. Naked
was the only way to get it, to slither the climate change
from those knee-high uplands to the *altiplano*

that waited for mother between the iron barred
headboard and footboard draped with his trousers.
She was outside that frame, on a stool
peeling stockings from her ankles.

Was it consternation on her face
as she struggled to unhook the first from her toes?
We were oblivious. All colour in that bedroom
leant towards the holiness of browns:

walls, floor, hair, skin, stockings, even her nightdress;
nesting browns, with us just fledglings, too young
to prey, to get it, so we flew into the thermals
of cotton, opened our mouths and sang.

Fantasy of Hiding in the Greenhouse

after 'Greenhouse and Garden', 1937

Hilda Spencer hid in the greenhouse,
with the door open as she'd found it,
and a heavyweight string of onions
like a macabre knotting of shrunken heads
to duck behind. Here hung a smell
of chilled bulbs that masked the sting
beneath papery layers.

She wasn't divorced yet, not absolute,
but the severing was real. She could taste it,
that and the residue linger
of last summer's tomatoes.
She had no hand in growing them.
They were none of her business.
She wasn't sure what she was doing here,
wearing the skin of someone from the past,
like a ghost staring into the familiarity
of a garden lost forever, the life
that wandered in it lost forever.

It was as she remembered; untended grass,
the last petals of clinging blossom,
an up-ended flowerpot, and a half barrel
of bare compost waiting
for something new to gush forth.

Each Day a New Unexpectedness

Hilda's staying in Hampstead with her mother,
who wears black and complains about the money
Stanley owes, wants to know why the girls are not
invited to be bridesmaids at their father's wedding.
They both drink tea, lots of tea, eat cherry cake,
listen to the news. It's hard for Hilda to keep track.

Hitler's on the rise in Germany. There's civil war
in Spain: 4,000 children have arrived in boats.
Three weeks ago the Hindenburg blew up.
Two weeks ago, a new King. And today, Saturday,
29 May 1937, the man she took to be her husband
is marrying for a second time.

Hilda picks at the chintz of her armchair.
She would like to forget their own small ceremony,
that wedding present from the Behrends –
a tea set covered with parrots. She stacks the cups,
turns down the music, 'When Did You Leave
Heaven?', crackling on the wireless.

She walks to the window, looks out over Pond Street.
The last of the May blossom is drifting to the ground.
How can she know it will be worse than this,
much worse, a week from now, after the new bride
has tricked her into adultery with this bridegroom
who is no longer hers?

She thinks of her children, the daughters
she and that once-husband made. Thinks
of the thousands of children caught in losses
not of their own making, sent away,
not knowing where they are, who they are,
what strange language they must now learn to speak.

The Apple Gatherer

I was the first wife,
the one who flew to earth
with strong wrists that could paint for hours,
nurse a child, turn a mangle.
I gathered seeds in my artist's smock,
the best windfalls.

But she had scissors in her pocket,
clipped my babies' wings,
taught us all to drink vinegar.
And when she became the second wife,
I, wishing my hips to be brash like hers,
agreed to be the mistress.

He said he was married to us both,
bugger the law, love was bigger.
Now I don't know which ring belongs where,
whether to be jealous of myself or her,
who's the mother of these step-children,
whose heart is barren.

I lie down in Cookham's orchards,
look up at apple trees he painted
when we lived in heaven.
Try to remember where I came from,
swallow my own forked tongue,
watch cyanide turn slowly into blossom.

Cottage at Wangford

'I am painfully aware & need no reminder that unless I spend eight
months of the year on doing landscape I shall not have enough
to live on for the winter and spring.'
—Letter from Spencer, Wangford, 1937

Did she come into her garden to see how he was getting on?
He'd set up his easel by the far curve of a half circle lawn.
Did she find the canvas empty, and Stanley, staring, empty,

perhaps having one of those imaginary conversations
Patricia said he would have? Did she say something inane –
Not got started yet then, Mr Spencer?

Did he machine-gun her with words, this landlady,
as Patricia (glad to be shot of him) said he would,
knowing she'd be sympathetic, ignorant of the facts,

when she could get a word in, with a man
revisiting the cottage where he'd brought his first wife,
his honeymoon Hilda, twelve years before?

Only the day before, he posted a letter asking her to join him.
He knew she wouldn't reply.
Maybe he smoothed the pillow on which her head had lain.

Perhaps he put the curtains that she drew each morning,
to his cheek. Were they the same curtains? Did he gaze,
remembering, in the drawers where she placed her clothes?

He might have replied, *Look closely Mrs Lambert, I've sketched
shapes faintly, see. I'm just waiting for colour to come fill the sky,
each sandy brick, edging stone, petunia, blue blade of festuca…*

Scorpion

after 'Christ in the Wilderness: The Scorpion', 1939

Life. He's already felt its sting.
He had it in the palm of his hand
and he had to poke it.

He's entered the wilderness,
a room in Hampstead; somewhere
to banish those mortifying erotic fantasies
that saw him stung.

Now he knows how venom tastes.
In sepia he reflects on scorpions
he'd seen before in the landscapes
of Macedonia.

*

His fasting Christ is corpulent,
shaggy-haired and bedded
into the world he loves

with its valleys, sharp stones and living beauty,
creations, like the one with a devil's tail
that tours the hillocks of his upturned hand.

*

He's on the edge of the bath,
facing the toilet, sketchbook angled on his lap.
He's been staring at bare floorboards,
breathing in all the smells.
It helps.

III. Summer Without Fire

He Taught Them Many Things
by Parables

after 'Village Life, Gloucestershire', 1940

Rationing has begun. And he paints himself
with two women (always two) –
Hilda, staring out of the frame,
and Daphne, dominatrix, taller than them both,
her arms across her bosom in disdain.

He brushes pin-stripes on his three-piece suit,
the golden tassel fringing Daphne's top,
keeps Hilda's sideways scowl, a sleeping dog,
a waiting-to-be-harnessed cart. None of them
connects with the add-on from a different sketch
where landlord Walter Stafford helps unpeg
the laundry, while his cleaner from *The White Hart*
folds the sheets. The bleached cotton (their stains
of love removed) has turned into the shirts of angels,
and Walter's grandson in his pre-school dress
is a young prophet pointing to the skies.

Paintings, Stanley fancies, are like dreams,
their meaning not always in the foreground
but in hidden details rarely noticed
at first glance. He's thinking of his first real oil,
Two Girls (yes, always two) *and a Beehive* –
where the holy ghost, easy to mistake
for clouds and sunrise, slides behind railings.

And here a corpulent body is camouflaged
behind a tree, as if smuggled from those canvases
of Christ in the wilderness. See how he bends
to clear the stony ground, plant row after row
of war-time leeks and cabbages.

She Doesn't Know How
He Had that Power

after 'Daphne', a portrait of Daphne Charlton, 1940

She was reduced to tears each day on purpose.
Nobody else could make her cry to order.
He wanted emotion, under the Bond Street hat.
Three guineas he paid for that, funeral black
with its pink rose and charcoal lace. Too much.
A perfectly good one may have been bought
           for much less than a pound.

But there she was that April, in Hampstead,
in the drawing room on the first floor, weeping
daily for maybe three weeks while he bickered
over her pale skin, fussed over the tilt of that hat,
the placing of her hair about the shoulders,
the folds in her blouse, and the curtains
           reflected in the mirror.

And here she is looking back at herself
from a face more than twice as old.
That mantelpiece bowl is still where it was.
The blouse she wore is in her wardrobe.
She can picture him squinting, nose near to canvas
as he copied its pattern, red and white floral
           on grey.

Her eyes are less bright, her lips not so full
and her cheeks have lost the porcelain glow
he gave them, the ones he would kiss lightly
           to bring her round.

In Port Glasgow...

'As I write this recitation of shipyard artworks, I am hearing
all sorts of mental harmonies, like listening to a Brandenburg.'
—Letter, Stanley Spencer, May 1940

the music begins quietly, contemplative: cup chinking saucer,
water slosh in a bowl, knock of a bar of soap re-seated in its dish,
scrape of razor, muted rasp of towel, a walk in chill air
with a chance of birdsong and street corner voices
berating the war or a husband's procrastination.
Hardly any of this achieves a full fortissimo,
or runs faster than a march.

As he passes the shipyard gates, there's percussion. The weight
of notes is earnest, even before it starts to rattle his ears
as he nears the source where steel pounds rivets
with an undertow tap of smaller hammers, sudden rips
from biting drills and the spat curses of welding torches;
fragments stitched like a quilt by men's dirty laughter,
bugger its and hollered advice.

The artist, the odd man in, finds one of his cosy spots,
elevated above the bees' nest of large oxidising pipes
and these rusty faces. He starts to unfurl
a new roll of waxy wartime toilet paper;
a fitting sketchbook for lean years,
for such a panorama of sound.

Summer Without Fire

after 'The Alder Tree, Gloucestershire', 1941

There's no one, no cries of agony, harsh words,
sombre wireless voice crackling as it unscrolls
bad news in received pronunciation, no drone
from the sky.

This corner of a Gloucestershire farm,
this wartime June smells of warm moss and nettle.
Elders curl over the stone tiles of a sprawling out-building,
like breaking waves in a profusion of white surf.

The artist has put himself on a rise among herbage.
Occasional white butterflies cut across his view.
Everything's in a hurry to fruit.
Blackberries are already the size and colour of peas.

He wants to paint it all: earthiness, warp and buckle,
simple acts of outdoor labour echoed in an upended cart.
He's admitting no one.
The sunlight he spreads on corrugated tin is his.

I Love Thinking about you Ducky

after 'Sketch of Hilda and Stanley', 1941

It's animal, not just an old term of endearment.
He even draws himself as a farm bird,
pecking distance from her dog-face contentment:
a deity for his adoration.

And below, on that same paper lined for words,
he fashions himself piggish, her cow-like;
a meeting of flat-nose, fat-nose.
He licks at her pink lips,

never denigrates beasts of the field
or their ways of love. They all have souls,
so it bothers him to hear *that a walk
was splendid because the walker didn't see one*,

as if blind to the eye to eye with sheep
and birds in a field, to the vitality
of trees (even naked ones) in woodland,
and deaf to all the songs that issue from them.

Truth and Lies in Port Glasgow, 1944

When he first came in June, he stayed one night only
because he had to share a bed with a film crew lad.

He'd no interest in the film being made.
They reduced him to monochrome,

put him where they wanted, pecking at a pencil
in places he would otherwise never go:

the top of a crane cab, high on a half-built ship,
or so far out on a breakwater,

that he was almost walking the Clyde.
The producer said it was where he liked to go,

put himself, dangerous positions in the wrong clothes,
shirt, tie, V-neck pullover, jacket and unsuitable shoes.

He didn't see them often, the clapper-board crowd,
but they'd overlay his steps with a Pathé-News voice.

The producer said he shifted about the yard
like a little bird. What could he mean?

Robin? Blackcap? Tit?

The Furnace Man

after 'The Furnace Man', 1945–50

Frank Chalmers is backed against a wall.
He dips his cloth-capped head. It's his pose.
He won't fasten to the eyes of the sketcher,
won't catch his gaze for long.
                              He's not fussed
with analysing nature's laws beyond the physics
of high temperatures on metals, those inside,
where the all day dissonance of caulkers,
riveters, welders and burners is familiar music.

It's muted here. His shovel's rested.
He's like cooling steel – tough, uncomplicated,
knows what he likes, what's expected from a day.

He'll even let you sit on his coals to dry
if you get wet. He's easily amused –

lucky to keep such wild wires for eyebrows.

The Psychiatrist

after 'The Psychiatrist', a portrait of Charlotte Murray, Glasgow, 1945

He doesn't paint her nude (mustn't flaunt the fact they're lovers),
but in the baggy comfort of her husband's dressing gown,
gold and grey and charcoal, with a pink cardigan beneath.
Her mouth's serene enough, but her eyes
are hemmed with black, as if Stanley knows

she's up to her neck in other people's shadows.
She chose this work so she could be like Virgil,
leading patients downward but always to the light.
The soul, or psyche, she fancied as a delicate,
transparent thing, linked with winged messengers

who aim towards ultimate benevolence.
Yet she, too, is dumbfounded as the last six years
reveal their still-born horrors one by one:
the brutal incandescence of those fires
beneath tall chimneys, the darkness. Some days

she is ashamed to be human, let alone German.
And she finds herself envying Stanley, being an artist.
Lesser mortals – or greater – would have been
thrown by Hilda's breakdown, Patricia's malice,
the century's *catalogues raisonnés* of pain.

But Stanley is able to be that bit of God
who goes on creating, no matter what.
Death does not exist for him, so there's less need
to grieve. Each painting is a new home,
an air-raid shelter, a resurrection where angels

converge with people, talk, knit, wind wool.
He pays close attention to the patterns on cushions
behind her: a thick white tulip upheld by a stem of blood,
a wheel of life, candy-striped, like the sweetness they've lost,
as if he'd paint out the swastika, paint in light's ghost.

Another Kind of Addiction

Spencer's 'Cookham from Englefield', 1948, was stolen from
Cookham Gallery in 2012, and recovered in 2017. The thief,
a drug addict, received a prison sentence.

It was hardly worth doing time for.

He didn't even find it beautiful –
the clouds sheepish,
Berkshire hedges over-clipped.
A fir tree had to stretch
to fill the space.

Perhaps the artist too
was strapped for cash.
Perhaps he too lived in terror
of being alone on a street corner,
his collar futile in the wind.

Perhaps he had his own sense
of unworthiness,
some great remorse
he needed to brush away.

Clever, though, to make it
too difficult to sell.

Clever, to make emptiness
seem so full.

Bloodrush

after 'The Glen, Port Glasgow', 1952

The world is so much better upside down.
You can hang hinged at the waist, dangle on
the rail by the canal till your fingers
grow numb. You can tread the grey sky, study
the dimpled flesh of your knees. You can smell
the pavement, watch the shuffle of ankles
and calves. You know what it is to be fat

and fluid as an atom. You glimpse hems
of skirts, an artist, someone's potatoes.
And now a woman near you starts to tip
forward, grip the rail, push her wide backside
into the air. Blood rushes to her head
as if she'd somersault over herself.
Grown-ups too can have enough of faces.

Dinner on the Hotel Lawn

after 'Christ Preaching at Cookham Regatta:
Dinner on the Hotel Lawn', 1957

We must get the cutlery right, lay clean linen cloths,
tables he can't overturn. We must hide love letters
behind our backs, though surely he knows everything:
how the earth will one day turn to pebbles,
the Thames to dishwater. We must remember
to thank him for the kind weather, daisies underfoot,
pelargoniums in pots, the miracle of white sliced bread,
tinned fruit and salmon. We must give one last spit
and polish to our spoons, then sit and shine
like marigolds waiting to be picked, our clothes
the colour of barley sugar. We must stretch our arms
as wide as a crucifix, undo our hearts,
pluck feathers from our heads that he might believe
he is once again in the company of angels.
And someone must paint a picture, capture the scene,
so on our death bed we may point to it, remind him,
'This is the day you promised we would be with you in heaven.'

Roy

after 'Roy', a pen and ink sketch of 1907,
and the painting 'In Church', 1958

Here's the ghost of a boy.
Fifty-one years on, still just tall enough
to reach over a pew. Roy Lacey,
young brother of a friend, boat builder's son,
first drawn grainy as the pew he leans over:

The congregation in organ-pipe conformity
won't flail arms as shown,
but being stiff with pride, will fail to notice him,
their flattery saved for their chorister kin.
Sometimes that reaches overflow, tumbles off lips.

Well done. Roy's been flung
to an outermost edge. He doesn't know he died
aged eight in 1910, but here he is recalled,
the cobwebs raked, torn, the lad-hair brushed
to conker shell shine,

reflecting that small sketch, that woody fuss
of lines and curves, broken
where God's light falls on hair and skin,
to make apertures that let what felled him in.

Self-Portraits: First and Last

after 'Self-Portraits', 1914 and 1959

In the kitchen of Wisteria Cottage, Cookham,
his first selfie, his big head painting, where he looks
beyond the physical into a mirror tilted slightly
to emphasise jaw and mouth. He's drawn

to this room where the light of a hot summer
streams in through windows looking east,
the only way he likes them, and yet, he puts
himself in the dark, chiaroscuro for drama;

an emergence into light from the darkness
of childhood and non-recognition. This painting
of oneself is a new idea. He says he's nervous,
doesn't want to speak about it. It'll take him a year.

*

In the house of Joy and Dennis, good friends
and patrons, from Dewsbury, Yorkshire, he stares
at us; one last reflective gaze out of canvas.
He has cancer and a bowel resection. He hides it well.

He's been dubbed Sir Stanley by the Queen Mother.
That was just a week or two ago, before he began
to build a craggier landscape of his face,
showing hair unbrushed, glasses slightly askew.

Now he knows what he sees.
Newspapers say he's painting this on his knees.
It's not true, but he must press on.
He's painting from the light towards darkness.

IV. Hilda with Bluebells

Hilda, Unity and Dolls

following her divorce from Stanley, in 1942, Hilda
suffered a breakdown and spent time at Banstead
Mental Hospital, Epsom. 'Hilda, Unity and Dolls'
had been painted by Spencer in 1937.

Throw me at the wall.
I am carmine, carnelian,
cobalt, ultramarine.
I am soot, opaque pieces
of pigment trying to float their way
into his fat figures
of Christ
of Judas
to step back into that portrait
he did of the four of us –
me in grim-looking spectacles,
Unity and two of her dolls.
Unity.
The name didn't work.
We still split up.
I split up.

Think of me when you see him
pushing that black pram
round the streets of Cookham
laden with easels, canvas, oil.
That was my girls' pram.
It was where they were rocked to sleep.

I could climb into it, my bones crushed
into paint, sepia coloured ash.
He could transform me
into one of his moon-faced saints.

Seated Nude

after 'Portrait of Hilda', 1942

It's an awkward study,
the light playing over me
as if I were sitting under a trellis –
beautiful but sad –
my flesh serene in its mortality.

Nipples erect, but only with the cold.
There is no lust,
none of the meaty pleasure
that reddens his portraits of Patricia.
My hips discreet,
my body haunted by promises
given then kissed away.

I allowed it all to happen
because I too saw the skies open,
the graves spilling their dead,
the veil of the temple rent.
Few painters can capture that, but he did.

Not me. I had babies instead – his –
and now my body is an empty vessel.
Please cover it.
Place a blanket over me.

He writes to me now, says he wants me back,
but the separation has settled around me
like silence I've grown used to.
My anger squashed like pressed flowers,
the flesh around my waist puckered.

Hilda with Bluebells

Spencer would paint 'Hilda with Bluebells' in 1955,
five years after Hilda's death

Still awake at 4 a.m. she thinks of herself
as one of those ruined abbeys – Tintern,
Rievaulx – her armpits arches that no longer know

how to hold up her shoulders, her head
a huge stone lying like a cannon ball
by the high altar. She's once more walking

down the nave on her wedding day, a woman
who will never stop painting, who wonders
if she should have chosen the other brother.

So many invisible lives threaded
through the eye of this one – children
she might have had, different sunsets –

but, for now, grief which has pushed her off
the shelf of herself, a body which has seeded
cancer. God appears in a maelstrom of gold,

long tentacles of light trying to yoke her back
to a sun that has forgotten how to hold
things together, everything in pastel,

easy to erase or smudge. When she sleeps,
she dreams of Stanley, of dying before him,
hauling him through gardens of love –

even, perhaps, forgiveness – and he is painting her
solid as a mother who has crawled back from death
to kneel amongst bluebells in her yellow dress,

soil sticking to her legs, hands foraging for something
she's lost, eyes in her heart-shaped face looking askance,
as if wishing she belonged in a different canvas.

A Ward Sister Remembers
the Spencers

Banstead Mental Hospital, Surrey, where Hilda stayed from
June 1942 to March 1943, was also used for the armed forces.

Each morning I would walk from the wounded
military – men missing eyes and limbs –
to the hidden wounds of patients, women mostly,

whose minds were absent without leave,
wandering somewhere in search of children,
husbands, front rooms they could no longer find.

I poured endless cups of tea from vessels
the size of watering cans, smuggled
snake's head and blue scabious from the downs.

Nothing surprised me. I knew every recipe
for breakdowns, every straw of a cure.
I watched minds wobble like penny farthings,

nights bulge with fear, women who traced
shapes on some invisible canvas,
their hands rising like redstarts in the air.

Hilda did that, I'm sure: painted the future
in her head: peace, Paris, laurel bushes,
her daughters by the sea. She talked a lot

to God, and Sundays were her favourite,
when Stanley visited and she could forget
human love is as flimsy as cardboard.

They sat in her room – her 'cell' she called it –
looking out at the world as if it were
the first garden, where they might pick lilies

of the field. And as I recall treatments
that were to come, I wish all my patients
could have saved their temples from electricity

as Hilda did, turning those wilderness months
into pastels of girls in woodland glades,
God in heaven, a golden oriole singing in a tree.

Re-Reading Stanley's Letters
and Thinking of Hilda

How boyish his love of bread and butter and marmalade,
his worship of beehives, ants, tortoises.

How often he meets himself in an *'unexpected way'*,
able to climb lamp-posts, rise from the dead.

And how *'chunkful'* he is of the Holy Ghost, *'the performance
of his love'* upon him, the glory of his Lord all around him.

I hear Patricia saying to him 'Stanley, you are not balanced.
Hilda is more balanced.' And here's Hilda sitting in her room

in Pond Street, trying to make sense of it all, talking
to God, with moons and visitations no one knows about.

She slides into depression the way a wife of Moses
might take refuge behind a waterfall to escape

the struck rock, the burning bush. She rarely paints
now, but remembers what Henry Tonks taught her

at the Slade: to keep practising the shape of eggs –
the way they take a lifetime to perfect.

The Paintings that Didn't Happen

hang in a studio down a side street,
perhaps an old shop, the walls faded
around their frames – large canvasses, her best work,
undaunted by failure or the muzzle of gender.

At night, she dreams of finding them in an auction –
women who prefer secrets over sleep,
children's faces wiser than the Buddha.
They stare back at bidders like the soul seeks god.

Here are fig trees the size of houses,
fields of dandelion that never turn to seed.
She is especially proud of the flamboyant nudes,
gentle wrinkles on their everlasting skin,

swans rising from the river, almond blossom
falling onto lovers as they couple on the ground.

Royal Free Hospital, Hampstead, 1 Nov 1950

Spencer would paint 'The Marriage at Cana: Bride
and Bridegroom', 1953 and complete 'Love on the Moor',
with its effigy of Hilda, 1955

She's waning now. He's tired, shuts the door
as if to keep her spirit in the room,
walks along Pond Street to the corner house,
doesn't speak, spoons sugar into his tea.

When he arrives back at the ward, the staff
treat him much as any new widower.
But at the funeral there'll be whispers,
No, Hilda wasn't his wife any more.

So many days of waiting, yet he's missed
the important moment, failed to help her
stare death in the eye. He plans the paintings
he will do of her, raised high on a plinth,

naked, while he's crouched, clinging to her legs,
her thighs, shapely ankles. Or one of her
sitting at the Marriage of Cana, hips
white with hunger. And their huge bridal cake.

Nocturne

When Hilda dreams of the afterlife
there is no baggage of desire,

none of the babies, brides, anecdotes
which weigh down Stanley's heaven.

She opts for a more limited palette –
woad blue, argentine –

the effect of light on water,
one snowflake, a moving cloud.

Let them be buried separately.
Let Stanley be woken by pilgrims

walking over his grave,
seeking the tombs which open

to revenants
and midnight orgies.

She's tired of hyperbole,
tired of his whole world

of ideas, wants something less earth,
more tide and air – the simplicity

of breath on a window,
an absence

of narrative.
The nirvana, say,

of one of Whistler's *Nocturnes*,
barely suggesting

the Thames
in moonlight.

In Which Hilda Brings her Complaints to God

1

I am the artist with the broken brush
in her hand.

I am the one who sketches
dead violets.

I am the mother whose pram
fell down the steps.

I am the corpse
Stanley carries on his back.

I hang round his neck
light as a feather.

Why did you have him lie in the tents of the ungodly?

2

I have joined the caravan of women
in white, on the wrong side of the road,
the wrong side of the sky.

I don't sleep. Every night the same.
I count sheep, hundreds of sheep, running
to the slaughter.

I consider the lilies of the field.
I consider the mother I wanted to be.

3

Where are the rooms that built love round us?
Where are the horseshoes, the four-leafed clover?
Where is the summer sun streaming through muslin curtains?
Where is the milk and honey?

Where are my feet? Where is my breast?

Where is my basket of ripe babies?

4

I used to think he would love me
out of my solitude,
as you do.

But now I see he loves me only
in the before and after,

loves me as I was, rummaging in a chest
of drawers, climbing into bed,

loves me as I will be,
naked on the moor.

He dreams of welcoming me home –
splashes poppies on my dress,
tears open their bodies.

He likes to have his arms around the dead.

5

First he wanted marriage, then divorce,
then marriage again.

I wish I could be like him,
selfish, painting.

But I was the woman caught in adultery.
Adultery – with my own husband
after he'd married another woman's lover!

I cursed him, loathed him,
and the curse rebounded on me

as curses do.

Where was the angel to stand behind me
with his fiery brand?

6

Oh, my daughters.
My lovely daughters, given away
to my brother's wife's mother,
Minniehaha.

Where is their hair to braid, their hands to hold?
Where is the clothes horse, with their damp socks and knickers?
Where the piano and prayers?

Where were you, who said you loved children?

7

He will turn me into a goddess
after I'm gone. He will plump me up
with sheen on my stockings.

He will worship at the altar
of his new beatitudes.

It is so much easier to love a woman
when she's covered in ivy.

8

The public will forgive him.
The queen will reward him.
Arise, Sir Stanley.

A man who drove his wife to hide
like silverfish behind the wallpaper.

9

His shame in me makes me ashamed
to meet myself. I am heavy with failure.
How will I rise to the heavens?

Even your terrible brightness tortures me.

In this, as in many things,
my husband was wrong.

Resurrection is the worst prophecy.

10

I lie down where the bluebells are thickest.

My body curls away into illness.

I am the shape of a coiled fern,
the head of a violin.

11

What do I pack for the journey?

My wedding ring?
The finger where attachment
squeezed too tight?

12

I used to think that when I climbed the stile
from the churchyard towards the river,

your smile would spread like a blessing
across my face. I would see new worlds.

But now I am in your many arms,

I remember only the swans I painted
that year my brother, Sydney, died,

the sweet Thames as it flowed under
Cookham Bridge –

gave back wings, trees,

clouds, a line of empty punts,
a small boat waiting to sail.

V. Love's Return

Sewing on a Button

'all ordinary acts such as sewing on a button
are religious things and a part of perfection...'
—Stanley Spencer

She sucks the frayed cotton
so it will pass more easily
through the eye.

This is the eye of heaven.
Camels buckle to their knees.
Pans, fish crates, sacks of learning

crash to the ground. The button
is all that is missing from our lives.
All that is mislaid, forgotten. Love

left by the wayside. She passes her needle
through the holes a dozen times,
once for each disciple.

Winds round the base, sews through
with one cross, cuts the thread
with her teeth. The button holds.

Adam fastens his jacket. It is the first day.
We don our Sunday best –
collars, cuffs. It is the last.

Next door, the man hammering
a nail is from Palestine.
The woman carrying their child

is, perhaps, the mother of God.
The artist who pushes a pram
of paints down the High Street

is helping to coax the world
into being every moment –
now. And again *now*.

She threads another needle.
Her thimble pushes the light.
She stitches the world together.

John Donne Arriving in Heaven

after 'John Donne Arriving in Heaven', 1911

He knew it would be a melting, looking back
at the world as a place of icicles and clouds,
lilies of passion unmooring their tangled roots.

Knew that with the rungs of prayer and reason
knocked away, the subtle knot undone,
he would step into this delicate permanence,

the light cleansing, as protracted evening sun
perfects a field of harvest corn.
Expected such radiance that finds no flaws

in all that's happened, no severity,
only the mercy of a paradise always autumn,
its joy possessed, ripe, perfect, complete.

But this is less the arrival he foresaw
than an undoing of distances, a shedding
of himself to become who he already was,

not gaining union but losing the illusion
he was separate, was ever other than this one:
the hand that set all things in motion,

spread this equal light, made on a whim
the stars, the schoolboys, the unruly sun.
All love a dream of this. And now, as he takes on

the bliss, the infinite bliss his little deaths
on earth struggled to reach, he finds his words
at last translated to their proper tongue.

The Resurrection of Soldiers

after 'The Resurrection of Soldiers', 1928–29

White crosses push up, tumble,
sounding like happy gunfire
when they clatter into and on top
of each other to become the new fallen.

Is there something in the air,
a chill or maybe a certain level of humidity,
like for ants that take to the surface
all at once to show off their new wings?

What a joyous racket as those last earthly
impediments tumble, when the ground moves,
when the fill-in soil pushes out,
and soldiers emerge, shake hands.

Such an undoing of war,
that rising without revolution, greeting,
the shaking off of interment. Such warmth
in first words, in the arm that reaches across

a mule. Even they and tortoises are back,
confused but touched. It'll be like heaven
on earth when the upheaval subsides,
when there's a cleansing fire and clouds clear.

Colour will return as a slow bleed
to the land, sky, their cheeks.
Others will drop in covertly – womenfolk,
butterflies, some summer flowers.

Touch Paper

after 'Love Letters', 1950

'I love the sort of passionate "monotony" of my continual
writing to you... Each wish to write to you gives birth
to another wish to write to you... You would have found
my letter supply more reliable than your water supply.'
—Spencer to Hilda, 1941

Your words pressed tight
against my chest
till my skin burns
as if this paper
that has touched your body
been breathed on
by your breath
held close against your heart
beneath your flowered dress
carries the fire of the sun
in its great script
of longing
of excess
of perfect love
brought down to earth
made flesh
made womanly
made you.

Oh love letters
sweet heart letters
how short-sighted I've become
in my love of you
reading the lines so closely
heat rising on pages
milled from beech and pine
and river that you
slipping the next envelope

into my jacket pocket
are nothing but a blur
a muse without whose
words I cannot live
cannot breathe unless
you write me again
promise me
there is no future
without this writing in it.

Candle and Snow

after a 1957 letter from Stanley to Hilda,
who had died in 1950

To say what is under a good layer of snow
is difficult

the accident of my being here
you being there

snow falling with no regard for logic
falling over what went before

over all I meant to say
all that is difficult

its whiteness a trick
a new resting place

the shape over which what comes next falls
the next layer to be walked upon

which is to say that love
is difficult

the bridge between me here
and you there

a new kind of courtship
a new *us*

the freshly falling and the fallen on
a kind of snow.

Letter from Stanley to Hilda, May 1959

'My great losses in my life are my pictures and Hilda...'
—Stanley Spencer

I should have painted you that morning at Chapel View,
leaning on the fence in your flowered dress.
I should have delivered you to yourself,
my Resurrection girl – every second
a Lazarus moment, every painting in place
of a tombstone – my happiness in you
like my marriage to trees, a joy I never imagined,
that joined us to everything –
so much kiss between us, so much *yes*.

I was the lucky one. Art poured through me
like an alleluia, my God immanent,
keen to declare himself in every cabbage
and dustbin, pushing me out in all weathers
with my pram of paints. Yours kept himself aloof,
made life an illusion to be seen through,
suffered, so though we were equal in talent,
you were less prolific, caught – like many women,
I realise now – in claiming less.
This was the real difference between us.
This was what I could never redress.

Then errors like brush-marks to be undone.
Nudes that were not you. Folly I could not overcome.
Your look of rage and shame. Your face in a room
that could never be home.

But oh, the pleasure of paradise regained
(*the mercy of again!*)
when we were once more under the lamplight,
heads touching, reading from the same book,
you dusting off the darkness. And the light
that held us in its halo was nothing

if not the light of the world that burns away
hurt and guilt – the mountain of the bereft become
the hill of the blessed.

And the girls
(the mercy of our girls!)
who walked in from fields white in the sun,
hands filled with heartsease, meadowsweet.

How could I not devote myself to art
which redeems absence, which reveals things
always as if for the first time?
Returns you to me even now, sitting
in the fat armchair, sliding letters into my pocket,
(oh, the mercy of love letters!)
the shocking brightness of you, the goodness
of your solid arm and thigh.

Till we arrive at last in the same painting,
rising out of each other, as if we have just died
and are to our astonishment come back
to taste the wonder of ourselves, the love.

In Cookham Churchyard

He too stood here once, on this very spot,
painting. The same yew trees, the same flint tower.
Tombs leant towards him in the soft summer
as the dead woke in their vaults, unquiet,
hungry for an afternoon such as this,
when jackdaws stalk the grass. Now his relics
lie under glass in the gallery: specs,
brushes, Bible open at *Lazarus*.

Of the disciples, he's most like Thomas,
wanting to touch the miracle of hands
which have worn death yet stay warm. And here stands
the stone angel he drew, lichened witness
to those crowded scenes of resurrection –
how, hour on hour, he painted love's return.

When I Think of Him in the Afterlife

he's pushing his pram of paints
in the empty streets above Cookham,
and a flurry of snow is starting to fall.

He's here to take stock, to weigh
the worth of his work against a life
clumsy in love. But he grows impatient

with all the whiteness – so much less glorious
than the resurrections he's imagined,
with their fat beatitudes. And where's Hilda?

Waiting, surely, wanting to wrap him
in her forgiveness. But no, no matter
how deep in the blizzard he goes,

he doesn't find her. And so he turns his back
on this cold heaven to race after her –
whoever she is now, woman or man –

that they might meet again in the world
where his unlove began, see it undone.

Resurrection: Reunion

after 'The Resurrection: Reunion', 1945

'Each individual in this picture is rising into a world
which is just the kind of world he or she wanted.'
—Stanley Spencer on his 1924 'Resurrection'

And suddenly they are streaming back from the dead,
unburying themselves,
their tombstones mere props for gossip
now the final day has come.

Only this is not the last day,
but the first of an eternal summer
where loss turns back into desire,
for what can match the pleasure of a kiss
on the tongue of those grown accustomed to tasting nothing?

Nothing more glorious for those whose senses were lost
than these arms around the loved one's shoulder,
the conjugal embrace, the breasts
that never bruise with too much touching,
the heavy angels spilling out of windows and doors
to welcome them home.

This is what they dreamt of ascending to –
gardens, allotments, lamps pooling light over dinner.
This what they longed to recapture –
reaching round a chest that rises and falls,
the rapture of breath that doesn't stop.

Flesh ripe with joy now they are touching again –
lovers, mothers, children, fathers, plumped-up wives –
in this light that is never switched off,
these bodies that cannot have enough of each other,
this love that is always being made.

The Heaven That Runs
Through Everything

'I want to bring all my pictures together
at the end of my life & look at them altogether.'
—Letter from Spencer to Henry Lamb, 24 October 1913

'Religion as I mean it is implicit in everything as a heaven
passing through everything...'

Here's to the small everyday miracles –
Mrs Baggett with her knitting and pearls,

the lovely daughters of Jerusalem
in their gardens of lilies, laburnum,

gospels and gossip at the regatta,
Sarah Tubb and her heavenly visitor,

courting and baptism along the Thames,
a dustman leaping into his wife's arms.

Here's to tulip, rock rose, gypsophila
flowering together, to vases of prayer,

Saint Francis in slippers and dressing gown
up on the roof with hens to catch the sun,

chores doing themselves down in the kitchen
at a wedding where water's turned to wine,

everything married to everything else –
yearning to show itself as happiness,

as Love. Neighbours who rejoice with tin cans
and cabbage leaves, the ripe summer commons,

skies which open over bulrush, goose-run,
the fresh light making everything new-born,

shot through with flame, each shrub a burning bush
by the tow path. All detail the flourish

of nature to show itself exactly –
not 'bird' but swan, cockerel, grebe, quail, turkey.

Blessings on Ricket's Farm, Rowborough, Pound Field,
the very word 'Eden' changed, now *this* world

is all we need to know of paradise.
Consider the gardens at Cookham Rise

where Adam's walking backwards to a tree
laden with unpicked apples – the first day

and the last become one, as if heaven was
wanting to reveal its eternal *Yes* –

earthly desire become beatitude,
everything known to be equally god.

Suffering a page to be folded over,
tenderness up sleeves in the tents of war,

balm poured from seraphs in the guise of men.
Nothing that is not transfiguration –

the dying girl next door raised up, restored
to life, then the quickening of a horde

of spirits, hungry for what death waylaid –
the lost embrace, words not said, love not made.

Here's to grief unlearnt, grateful breath redrawn,
the rapture of rolling away the stone.

And let's not forget the man most at home
in sunlight, newly arrived in Cookham,

who walks with disciples up Cockmarsh Hill,
everyone in the crowd a plump angel.

Chronology of Lives
of Stanley Spencer and Hilda Carline

1889   Nov 20 Birth of Hilda – Annie Hilda Carline – London
1891   June 30 Birth of Stanley, 8th surviving child of William
        and Annie Spencer
1903–8 Hilda attends Oxford High School
1907   Stanley attends Maidenhead Technical School
1908–12 Still living in Cookham, Stanley attends Slade School of Art
        London, entrance exam waived
1910   Stanley's first serious attempt at oil painting: *Two Girls
        and a Beehive*
1913–16 Hilda attends Tudor-Hart's School of Painting, Hampstead
1914   War declared in August. Stanley joins Maidenhead branch
        of Civil Guard and St John's Ambulance Corps
1915   Stanley meets Hilda's brother Richard Carline
        July Stanley enlists in Royal Army Medical Corps and works
        as an orderly at Beaufort War Hospital, Fishponds, Bristol
        (formerly a lunatic asylum)
1916–18 Stanley on war service in Macedonia. Hospitalised with malaria
1916–19 Hilda works for the Land Army
1918   Stanley returns to Cookham
1919–24 Hilda studies part-time at Slade School of Art
1919   Dec Hilda and Stanley meet at a Carline family dinner,
        Hampstead, through her brothers Richard and Sydney
1922   Sydney Carline becomes Drawing Master at Ruskin School, Oxford
        Stanley joins Hilda on a painting holiday in Yugoslavia;
        he proposes for the first time
1924–26 First Resurrection paintings
1925   Feb 23 Hilda and Stanley marry at Wangford Parish Church
        Nov Birth of Hilda and Stanley's first daughter, Shirin
1926   Dedication of Sandham Memorial Chapel, Burghclere
1927   Stanley's first one-man exhibition at the Goupil Gallery;
        the Tate buy *Resurrection, Cookham* for £750
        The Spencers move to Burghclere where Stanley works
        on a series of war paintings in the Chapel

1928	They move to Chapel View Cottage. Elsie Munday is the family maid
	Stanley and Hilda meet Patricia Preece and Dorothy Hepworth
	Spencer's work shown at Venice Biennale, also in 1930, 1932, 1938
1929	Death of Hilda's brother Sydney
1930	May 24 Birth of Hilda and Stanley's second daughter, Unity
1931	Spencers return to Cookham
1932	Stanley starts a relationship with Patricia Preece
	Dec Death of Hilda's brother George
1933	Shirin moves to live permanently with Mrs Harter, Hampstead
1934	May Hilda and Stanley separate
1935	Royal Academy rejects many of Stanley's paintings, including *St Francis and the Birds*
1936	One-man exhibition of his paintings with his dealer, Dudley Tooth
	Hilda begins divorce proceedings
1937	May Decree absolute of Hilda and Stanley's marriage
	May 29 Stanley marries Patricia Preece
1938	Oct Stanley leaves Cookham; lives in North London
	Christ in Wilderness series
1939	Outbreak of war
	Unity moves to live with Shirin and Mrs Harter in Epsom
	Stanley starts affair in Leonard Stanley with Daphne Charlton (wife of George Charlton, teacher at Slade)
	Commission from War Artists' Advisory Committee to paint series of pictures of shipyards in Scotland
1940	Stanley begins painting at Port Glasgow
	Stanley's affair with married Jungian psychiatrist Charlotte Murray
	Shirin and Unity evacuated to Lynmouth, Devon
	Hilda's friends, Constance Oliver and Eddie Pearson, killed in the Blitz
1942	Stanley exhibits at Leicester Galleries
	Hilda enters Banstead Mental Hospital, Surrey for 9 months, Stanley visits her once a week
1943	Hilda moves back to Finchley Road, Hampstead
1946	Nov Hilda visits Paris with Shirin and Richard Carline

1947	Hilda's breast cancer and mastectomy
	Behrends endow Sandham Memorial Chapel, Burghclere, to the National Trust
1948	Stanley begins unsuccessful annulment proceedings against Patricia on grounds of non-consummation of their marriage; they are later terminated
1950	Stanley made a member of the Royal Academy and awarded a CBE
	Unity enrols at the Slade
	Nov 1 Death of Hilda at Royal Free Hospital, Hampstead
	Spencer continued writing letters to Hilda until his own death
1951	Formal deed of Stanley's separation from Patricia; maintenance agreed
1955	Nov–Dec Tate Gallery First retrospective of Stanley Spencer's work
1959	July 7 Stanley's Knighthood at Buckingham Palace
	Dec 14 Death of Stanley from cancer; buried in Cookham Churchyard
1963	Opening of Stanley Spencer Gallery, Cookham
1963	May 13 Birth of Unity's son John
2017	Oct 18 Death of Unity Spencer

Two Rivers Press has been publishing in and about Reading
since 1994. Founded by the artist Peter Hay (1951–2003),
the press continues to delight readers, local and further afield,
with its varied list of individually designed,
thought-provoking books.